The Sayings of Imam Warith Deen Mohammed

Volume I (1975-1981)

ALLAH - U - AKBAR

Dedication

To

Vibert Muhammad III and Malik Lewis Muhammad and others who are striving in the way of Prophet Muhammad (Peace and Blessing Upon Him) and the Holy Quran

Contents

I

Authors

Vibert Muhammad is a faculty member in the History Department at the University of Central Florida. He is the premier scholar on the Nation of Islam and Islam among people of the African diaspora. His research has explored traditional and new schools of Islamic dogma throughout the Caribbean and Latin America. In addition, Professor Muhammad is a public historian who specializes in archeological history. His works has been shown on PBS, BBC, the History Channel, Discovery and several major networks such as NBC, ABC, and CBS. His scholarship also ranges into Afro-Latino Cultural History, Constitutional and Legal History and Labor and Social History

and African religions in the Americas. In addition, he is the author of hundreds of articles and the academic bestseller, Inside the Nation of Islam.
Dr. Muhammad has served as a minister in the Nation of Islam and currently serves as prison Imam under the Ministry of Al-Islam and the Islamic Society of Central Florida, Orlando.

Michelle Muhammad is a corporate manager and academic researcher. She is the steady aid to Professor Muhammad in the collection and management of data and their businesses. Sister Muhammad can be heard on Islamic radio shows and blogs nationwide. Her lectures and writings focuses on women in Al-Islam. She is the unofficial biographer of Sister Clara Muhammad, the wife of the Honorable Elijah Muhammad

Hatim Hamidullah is a servant of Allah (G-d), respected Imam of Masjid Al-Haqq in Orlando, Florida. He is also a member of the Florida Conference of Muslim Americans in association with the ***Ministry of Imam WD Mohammed*** and a member of the Shura of Imams of the ***Islamic Society of Central Florida.*** Imam Hamidullah is also on ***The Mayor's Interfaith Executive Council of Central Florida.*** Imam Hamidullah is the Executive Directive and co-founder of ***Knowledge for Living, Inc.*** a timely and fast growing 501C nonprofit organization which seeks to improve the total wellbeing of citizens in economically disadvantaged communities. He has held responsible positions as Imam for many years. Imam Hamidullah was selected as a guest of the ***Kingdom*** of ***Saudi Arabia*** to participate in the first intensive Islamic Educational program in Washington DC, consisting of subjects such as arabiyyah (Arabic), hadith methodology, (seerah history), and fiqh (religious rulings). His travel includes Saudi Arabia, South Africa, Spain, Morocco, and Canada. Imam Hatim is a frequent lecturer throughout the United States as Masaajid, Universities, Colleges, Churches, Synagogues, and adio stations, email-hhamidullah@hotmail.com

ALLAH-U AKBAR

II

Introduction

The late Imam Warith Deen Mohammed led the American Muslim Mission, formally known as the Nation of Islam and later the World Community of Al-Islam from 1975 to 2008. Born Wallace Muhammad, the seventh child of the Honorable Elijah Muhammad who led the Nation of Islam from 1933-1975.

Under the leadership of Imam Mohammed the Nation of Islam evolved to become a complete universal Muslim community that emerged to accept Quran and the traditional principles of faith that is based on the Sunna (teachings) of Prophet Muhammad (PEACE AND BLESSINGS OF ALLAH BE UPON HIM).

Leading the largest American Muslim community in the United States Imam Mohammed promoted the virtues of Islam in every corner in the United States. He became the first

Imam to pray before the United States Congress and the only one to have been invited to the White House to meet American presidents. Under the Imam's ministry he continued to fight for the rights of African-Americans, minorities and the oppressed while testifying of the nature of Al-Islam as being a religion of peace, love, and progressivism.

Following in the traditional voice and character of American Muslim leaders such as Noble Drew Ali, Fard Muhammad,

Malcolm X, Elijah Muhammad, and Louis Farrakhan; Imam Mohammed gave voice to the voiceless, hope to the hopeless, and strength to the weak while bringing the beauty of pure Al-Islam to North America.

In The Sayings of Imam Mohammed (Volume I) we attempted to capture elements of his wisdom, philosophy and theology in a manner that is palatable and applicable to our everyday living.

We pray and hope that you enjoy the read and that it will provide inspiration as you journey through life.

III

History of Imam Warith Deen Mohammed

Imam Warith D. Mohammed is one of the greatest leaders in the evolution of Islam in the United States. Born in Detroit October 30, 1933 to The Honorable Elijah Muhammad and Sister Clara Muhammad, Wallace grew up as a devout Muslim in the Nation of Islam. His father, also known as The Messenger, raised his son in two "schools" of Islamic thought;

one, that Master Fard
Muhammad was Allah in person
and the second "school," is that
the basic principles of Islam and
the belief in the Quran unites all
Muslims.

Wallace Mohammed was a
spiritual and clairvoyant child
who had an uncanny ability to
understand the Bible and Holy
Quran. According to his mother
Clara, Master Fard Muhammad,
prophesized that she would give
birth to child of extraordinary
spiritual clarity. Thus, when her
seventh son was born—the

Messenger and Sister Clara
named him after Fard
Muhammad, who also was
known as Wallace Fard
Muhammad.

In the Nation of Islam
Wallace closely studied the
teachings of Master Fard
Muhammad, the leadership of
his father, and the structure of
the Nation. In the late 1950s he
was among a unit of outstanding
young Muslim leaders such as
Malcolm X and Louis Farrakhan,
who would revolutionize Islam in
the United States and make the

Muslims a permanent pillar in Black America. In the 1950s the social landscape of the nation was going through a legal transformation. In 1954 the United States Supreme Court overturned Plessy v. Ferguson (1896) in Brown v. Board of Education of Topeka, Kansas maintaining that segregation was unconstitutional and that it bred inferiority in the minds of the African-American. However, Wallace Mohammed and the Nation of Islam held another position.

In 1958 as the minister of Temple 12 in Philadelphia, Wallace preached the Nation's line of separation and the development of a Black independent state. In addition, he voiced opposition to the nation's involvement in wars while urging African-Americans not to join the military. Leading by example, he refused to sign up for the selective services for military duty and boycotted the notion that he could receive special treatment in non-war duties as a conscientious objector. Instead, he accepted the nation's punishment for his refusal of military duty by going to federal prison.

In jail, following the advice of his father who was sentenced to prison for refusal to register for military service during World War II and Malcolm X who was convicted of burglary in the 1940s served his prison time studying American, Christian and Islamic histories. In the penitentiary, Wallace became aware of the Nation of Islam's teachings in new manner. He began to question the notion of Master Fard Muhammad's divinity and some of the contradictions in theology that the Nation had with traditional or Sunni Islamic doctrine. It should be noted, that Wallace was fluent in Arabic prior to his conviction. The Honorable Elijah Muhammad hired Professor Jamal Diab, a Palestinian to teach Arabic and Islamic culture at the organization's secondary school, The University of Islam. Diab often referred to Wallace as his most brilliant student.

After his release from prison Wallace returned to Philadelphia as the Nation's minister. However, he began to slowly incorporate several doctrines of Sunni Islam into the theology of the Nation of Islam. The inclusion of "new" doctrine to Fard Muhammad's teaching caused tension and concern in the Nation of Islam. According to Yusef Shah, former official of the Nation of Islam, who presented the Messenger with a recorded tape of Wallace's lecture to members of the Nation; the

Messenger smiled and said, "he's got it; but, it was not the time" to teach traditional Islam to our people. Wallace could not understand the reasoning of his father and continued to teach his "new found" truth of Islam. Ultimately, he was expelled from the Nation.

During the early 1960s Wallace was extremely close to Malcolm X, minister of the New York City Mosque and National Spokesman for NOI and the Honorable Elijah Muhammad. In 1963 Malcolm became of aware of the Messenger's wives and children. Trying to make sense of this revelation he questioned Wallace about his father's domestic life. Wallace confirmed that the rumors of the Messenger's life were true. Both men agreed that the Quran allowed for such actions; however, they began to question The Honorable Elijah Muhammad's leadership as the Messenger of God. Until the assassination of Malcolm X in 1965 the two men were constant associates and allies.

After the death of Malcolm, Wallace asked to be readmitted into the Nation of Islam; without hesitation The Honorable Elijah Muhammad allowed him to rejoin the group. Although Wallace was back into the fold; he never ceased his teachings of Sunni doctrine inside the group's temples. In fact, The Messenger never attempted to stop him. He only encouraged the younger Muhammad to suspend this teaching for "a time."

In the later period of the 1960s and early 1970s the Nation of Islam had grown into the largest and wealthiest Black organization in the United States. Having a net worth of over $300 million dollars that claimed ownership of the largest Black newspaper in the country, apartment buildings, grocery stores, secondary and high schools, banks, medical centers, shopping centers, trucking firms, multiple homes, farms, restaurants, a fast food chain, planes and foreign trade activities with a membership now in the millions the Nation of Islam was truly a nation within a nation. In fact, scores of white businessmen flocked to Chicago to see the Messenger to ask of opportunities for investment. In which, he always refused saying, "the Nation of Islam is not for sale."

In late 1974 Wallace Mohammed at Temple 7 at a Fruit of Islam meeting in New York openly announced his contexture of Islam and how the Nation would operate under his leadership. In February, one day before Savior's Day, the Nation's yearly convention the Honorable Elijah Muhammad had expired. On February 26, 1975, one day after the announced death of The Messenger the Nation of Islam conferred Wallace Mohammed as the Supreme Minister of the Nation of Islam; thus, marking a new era in the history of Islam in the United States.

The leadership of Wallace Mohammed evolved the Nation into a spiritual center that aligned perfectly with the Honorable Elijah Muhammad's vision of being an Islamic community of independence and self-determinism. While he physically altered the appearance of the Nation such as the changing of his name to Imam Warith D. Mohammed and the Nation of Islam to The American Muslim Mission; the real transformation was in his philosophy and theology of connecting the struggle of African-Americans with the traditional tenets that are found in Al-Islam. You will find in <u>The Sayings of Imam Warith D. Mohammed</u> that the Imam was a brilliant thinker, teacher and twentieth century mujahidin—a divinely appointed Muslim world leader. Indeed, Imam Mohammed, a humble and sincere man whose words always carried wisdom, comfort, and strength. Read, enjoy and reflect.

Excerpt From Prophet Muhammad's Farewell Address

O people! Lend an attentive ear to my words; for I know not whether I shall ever hereafter have the opportunity to meet you here. Do you know what today is? This is the sacred Day of Sacrifice. Do you know what month it is? This is the sacred month (Dhul-Hijjah). Do you know what place this is? This is the sacred town (Mina). So I inform you that your lives, properties and honor must be as sacred to one another as this sacred day of this sacred month, in this sacred town. Let those who are present take this message to those who are absent. You are about to meet your Lord, Who will call you to account for your deeds. As of this day all sums of interest are remitted, including that of Abbas ibn Abd al-Muttalib. Every right arising from homicide in pre-Islamic days is henceforth waived, and the first such right that I waive is that arising from the murder of Rabi'ah ibn al-Harith ibn Abd al-Muttalib. O people! this day Satan has despaired of re-establishing his power in this land of yours. Nevertheless, should you obey him, even in what may seem to you trifling, it will be a matter of pleasure for him. Beware of him, therefore, for the safety of your religion.

Source: Prayer and Al-Islam

Imam Warithdudin Muhammad

IV

The Savior

The Honorable Elijah Muhammad saw Master Fard Muhammad who came from the East and recognized him as the Savior.

The Bible says that our Savior would come from the East and tell us (Bilalians/ African-Americans) that we are also from the East.

Jesus said; I am the Son of Man.
Son of Man means being a
follower.

Instead of Christians following
what Jesus wanted them to
follow; they are doing the thing
that he tried to save them
from—the worshipping of
personalities.

We are here to remake the
world; not just the world of
temples, but the world of
America and the whole world
outside of America.

Christ means knowledge.

The Holy Quran calls Jesus a Kalimatian. Kalimatian means message, a sign or a word.

The name given to Prophet Muhammad(PBUH) in the Holy Quran means the one who received his knowledge or training from mother. This great prophet is called, "Prophet of Mother—Wit."

The Honorable Elijah Muhammad is my Savior as he is your Savior. He is our spiritual father.

Prophet Muhammad (PBUH) was not an angel! Allah said: "If the earth had been populated with angels, I would have sent you an angel as a Messenger."

Crazy spiritual ideas resulting from misreading the Bible split the human being and forget to put the other half back; thus, leaving many to think that we need an unnatural being to lead natural beings.

We don't believe in spooks.

The biggest mystery in religion is Christ and the "Man of Sin (Satan)." Satan is in a human body. Satan never affects man in a big way, except when he appears in a human body

Pray to only Allah—God.

The real believer is one who puts absolute trust in Allah. He does not doubt Allah to any degree or in any sense.

The Opening

Al-Fatiha

1. *With the Name Allah, The Most Gracious, The Most Compassionate.*
2. *Praise be to Allah, The Lord of all the worlds;*
3. *The Most Gracious, The Most Compassionate.*
4. *Master of the Day of Judgment.*
5. *You do we worship and your Aid we seek.*
6. *Guide us on the straight way.*
7. *The way of those on whom You have bestowed Your Grace. Those whose (portion) is not wrath, and who go not astray.*

NOTES

Some teachings in Christianity create an emotional being that does not respond to wisdom, knowledge and understanding.

The teachings of Master Fard Muhammad accomplished the revitalization of Islam and the revival of Islam in our physical life—a revival that manifested in the eating of proper foods, the wearing of proper dress and the speaking of Islamic language.

The Honorable Master Fard Muhammad used symbolic and mystical teachings and Black

Nationalism to remove the teaching of the genesis of the creation of the original man. He put Black man as the original man; not the so-called Caucasian. He reversed the psychology and with it he brought us to the practice of Islam in our lives.

When a person accepts Al-Islam and then leads a virtuous, pious life in accordance with its teachings, all his previous misdeeds are erased because he has proven his sincerity by putting forth earnest efforts towards his moral uplifting.

Repentance in Al-Islam means giving up sin and it requires a wholehearted change in thought and deeds. We should strive to rid our minds and hearts of remembrance of the pleasure of sin.

Taqwa is God-consciousness. Taqwa comes from a motivation to obey Allah and Allah is its constant object.

In the beginning your faith was not strong enough to motivate you to action, but the nearer you come to proper attitude and obedience in your worship of Allah, the stronger that faith becomes.

Allah describes Al-Islam as Din (Deen) Al-Fitrah, which means the religion established on the laws and principles which uphold creation.

The Christ comes to the world first as a savior and he is crucified. Then he returns as an executioner and judge, executing judgment on the world.

The resurrection of Jesus is what you are seeing today in the Nation of Islam (The Body of Christ).

The Bible tells us of two forces or two people or companies. One is describe as agents of Almighty God or saints of Almighty God or friends of Almighty God who go about in the earth searching the earth to find those that they can present to God as worthy.

The Bible teaches us that there is a time and a season for everything under the sun, then we as men and women of knowledge must first ask the question because our leader has taught us to think five times before we act, think five before we speak.

The scientist is born of knowledge. He is not born of what we can fashion from mud. He is born of knowledge and knowledge is like fire.

Bilal was a Black Ethiopian slave who was an outstanding man in the history of Islam. He was the first muezzin (minister) of Prophet Muhammad (May Peace Be Upon Him).

The great Masters Fard Muhammad and Elijah Muhammad lit the torch of Islam and the Islamic mentality has produced a clean righteous people who are contributing to the financial, social, economic, and spiritual upliftment of the total community.

The Honorable Elijah
Muhammad is telling us that the
new book that is to come is
really a new book to us because
we have never known the Holy
Quran. We have known the
Bible. Most of us know more
about the Bible then we know
about the Holy Quran.

The Honorable Elijah
Muhammad said; that there is
no better prayer service than the
prayer service of Islam.

The revolution brought about by
the Holy Quran was not just a

revolution which affected the physical environment. The pagan Arab tribes during the time preceding the revolution of the Quran had no regard for cleanliness.

The Lost Found Nation of Islam in the West (Body of Christ) has been blessed with the light of divine learning which has broken the seals on the mysteries and the hidden meanings of the Book (Bible) and the wisdom.

We do not know God in flesh and we do not know God in

symbol. We know God in knowledge.

Islam is a balance between the spiritual and material worlds.

Resurrection of the dead means to stand up on your intellect.

You cannot compromise Islam.

Allah never needs a rebirth, resurrection; he was never born nor will he die. God is forever.

NOTES

V

History

In America, our community
[Nation of Islam/World
Community of Al-Islam] began
with the teachings of Master
Fard Muhammad. When we say
"master" we mean "teacher."

Hypocrisy is rampant in the
history of America. Hypocritical
people led our marches and
stood out in front of us saying,
"We must free the Negro
(African-American), we must

give the Negro (African-American) his rights.

The first thing that we experienced in slavery was the destruction of our family.

The purpose of the World Community of Al-Islam in the West is the removal of falsehood and the restoration of pure Islam.

The World Community of Al-Islam in the West is an evolutionary change; without change society dies.

The so-called African-American has no real understanding of self. We have allowed others to identify and define us.

Your roots must be in human life; not in materialism.

We must become sensitive human beings; that is, to feelings, needs and love.

Ancient Egyptian mythology is Black African mythology.

Jesus and no other person have been more cruelly crucified

physically than the Black man of America.

No people in history had lost as much at the hands of the white man than the Bilalian (African-Americans).

Minister Malcolm was thrown out from among us by forces we did not know. I was thrown out by the forces. The Messenger was separated from his youngest son, Akbar Muhammad by these forces. We must identify and understand these forces.

Man is to blame for his sins and the wrongs he inflicts upon himself; the knowledge that we get out of the study or from the study of the physical world serves as light for the mind to show us that of the physical creation that the physical light cannot show us.

Master Fard Muhammad recognized our true history; he identified us as a people who were "lost" from our land, our people and our religion.

The Lost-Found Nation of Islam
in the West was established to
be a part of the great, vast,
universal Nation of Islam all over
the world. We want the world to
know that we are a part of the
Universal Nation of Islam.

VI

Leadership

It is not enough to be morally fit to lead, but we must also have the knowledge to lead.

Isolation was good for me; it made me make a job for myself. Do for self!

The salvation of society and the survival of civilization depend upon establishing and preserving healthy, sound, truthful and charitable leadership.

We must teach our youth how to lead using the principles of Islam.

Government can't reform society; only God can do the reforming.

Khalifah is an obedient follower to Allah; he is one who comes behind. Jesus said, "I must do the work of my heavenly father." He meant that he must fulfill the role of Khalifah. Khalifah is one who comes later.

We must be able to support, defend and establish our knowledge under any test.

The power is in the message of Islam.

Allah guides the believer who bows to him.

We can't follow individuals unless they take up the word of Allah and lead us with the banner of truth.

If you don't wake up today, you won't have another chance. Today is your last chance.

You can't grow into Supreme Wisdom until you understand the real purpose and nature of moral knowledge.

When great people stand up for right don't expect your open enemies to endorse them.

You can be very righteous conscious, but that does not mean that you are righteous. Self-righteous people only think of themselves as righteous, but they don't have an eye to see righteousness in others.

They know that Islam alone is the key to freedom, justice, equality and strength for the Bilalian (African-American) communities of the west.

Minister Farrakhan is a fine representative of the leadership of the Honorable Elijah Muhammad and the Nation of Islam.

The prophet needs warriors to stand up to attack supremacy and ignorance.

VII

Righteousness

Maryam, the mother of Jesus,
was a holy woman who was
raised in the schools of the
sacred scripture.

As Muslims, we must love the
Muslims life and accept the
great responsibility of serving
God and truth for the sake of all
creation. That means we must
accept to be the Khalifah of God.

Allah is not going to make life
pleasant for us until we first take

the right disposition in our hearts.

Submit yourself completely to Allah. Allah will not fail you. God is the compensator.

God conditioned you to benefit from his blessings.

Black people, Muslims; you have the capacity for moral superiority.

I am not asking you to be an Arab Muslim; I am asking you to be a Muslim under the prophet—Muhammad (PBUH).

Don't expect the world to join you in righteousness; you will have to pull the world to righteousness.

We cannot as Muslims pick up the ways of those people who are un-Islamic, or the ways of the oppressors who are inhuman.

The best people around me are crippled; give me the worst so that we can transform them for a great society and work.

Islam is the salvation for the world; the champion of freedom, justice and equality.

True religion has the courage, the compassion and the strength to do something about the people's needs. A religion of this kind is not seen in the western society, except in the work of the Lost-Found Nation of Islam in the West.

Religion is the salvation of humanity.

God chose us—the Black Muslim in America as his people.

Allah did not have to teach human beings a belief in something beyond the physical life. Human beings believe in something beyond the physical life, by nature.

The position of prayer refers to the Lost Found people of Islam. Before their return they must turn in the direction (Ka'ba) with clean hands and hearts, bow in submission to the will of Allah alone with the righteousness that they may be welcomed to take their place again among their own people.

The five prayers of the day are spiritual refreshment and he who cleanses himself in and out leaves no filthiness.

Every living thing born from the womb grows to stand over the womb as the preserver, protector and nourishes of the womb.

The Muslim is a giant in creation and he accepts the responsibility to pull up falling civilization or falling society.

When people come into the knowledge of the nature and

purpose of the moral teachings, they are truly liberated. That's what Jesus meant when he spoke of being made "whole."

We are slave servants of God and we are too great in our moral makeup and in our spiritual makeup to carry racial prejudices that are unnatural and that are not in accord with universal truth.

Muslims have the Ramadan fast as a protection for us. During the month, we learn to control the distraction, fiery passions of the biological nature.

The Muslim life is a full life, a balance life and life that accepts the challenge that God has given to us.

Allah will never deliver a people until they first change themselves.

Allah, God contains everything it is not in our power to grasp him in his entirety. The Holy Quran says that God is Al-Akbar, meaning that he is the bigger or the greater.

Al-Islam is more than a set of guiding principle—for Muslims it is a complete way of life.

The institution of prayer has been completely and perfectly established by Prophet Muhammad (PBUH).

Within Al-Islam there are groups which are guided by affluent schools of thought: Sunnis, Shi'ites, Malikis, Hanbalis, and Hanafis. We are all Muslims; we have faith in Allah.

A person who makes the Declaration of Faith, but who

brings about no change in his life has not accepted Al-Islam in his heart. He must put his faith into practice in order for it to revolutionize his life.

Our repentance is acceptable to Allah if we are sincere.

Repentance is Al-Islam means giving up sin and it requires a wholehearted change in thought and deeds.

A person who claims to be a Muslim, but hides his faith is not a believer.

The faithful Muslim fears losing his relationship with Allah and that saves him from spiritual ruin. He is a slave of Allah alone.

A faithful Muslim is one who believes in the oneness of Allah and in the consistency of the prophet-hood of his prophets. His heart is for righteousness. Any amount of unrighteousness troubles his heart.

In obeying Allah, we are respecting our relationship with everything in creation.

The root word of Al-Islam is "aslama" which means to enter into peace, or to submit.

You must accept your place in the Body-Christ (Nation of Islam), the Ummah, the community, if you want to be saved from the destruction of their world of grafted Caucasian mentality. We are the resurrected Jesus.

Right now we are living in a time when religion has been dead. Allah has blessed us with the presence of Divine Mind to bring the truth of religion to light before the world again.

True religious atmosphere is an atmosphere of intelligence, compassion, respect for one's self, and respect for each other, sympathy, self-value, and an understanding of the value of others.

VIII

Understanding

Today the world needs saving,
but what do they [Christians]
have to offer the world? They
can offer nothing but spiritual
exercises that are of no real
consequences or significance
when it comes to running the
world.

Arab Muslims and the Muslims
of the old world are helpless to
help the Black American.
America is hell; they are ill
equipped to handle this devil in

America. The Arabs are morally too weak to deal with this Lucifer.

The Muslim woman is a liberated woman in Islam and is not unprotected or neglected. The Muslim woman is a respected being. We value her for her role in society or as a mother and as the first womb of society. The woman in Islam is sacred to us and the ties of relationship are sacred.

Don't forget your share of this world.

A humble man is a happy man.

You will stay in a negative state until you change your attitude.

Work as though you will live forever; work as though judgment will be today.

By nature you are equal to anybody on this earth.

Because of our physical, moral and spiritual suffering under the rule of white supremacy under the rule of white supremacy, we are justified in [Allah's] eyes to stand up now as the liberated

Jesus from the physical cross to lead and to judge the world.

When people understand the message of Al-Islam and feel an obligation to declare themselves Muslims before Allah and before the Islamic community, their hearts are taking a courageous stand.

Caucasians will never respect you as long as you keep the names that their slave master parents gave you.

If we could get the 30 million Bilalians (African-Americans) in

North America to change their names (no matter what religion they believe in), there would be a revolution (change in white-black relationship) overnight.

Sensitivity and righteousness is based on total submission to God.

Islam compels men to provide for his family.

A halal life; is a complete life!

Every son of Adam is dignified. God created us in the most excellent design.

The Honorable Elijah Muhammad made you; made us; industrialist. I simply add spirituality to his teachings.

We are the only ones who can give moral leadership to the world. We are the ones who can sit as moral judges for the world. We know more about crimes because of our suffering and our experiences than any people on the face of the earth.

You should never push prayer out of your mind and say, "Oh, this is America, not an Islamic society." That is the first crack in your building. Very soon it will crumble and fall.

Today's generation need an Islamic revival.

God is not going to put bread in your mouth; he gave your hands to do something for yourself.

The development of faith within a human begins when his moral consciousness makes him aware of the need to be morally clean and truthful and to avoid things which are sinful.

Lost Found Nation of Islam in America [does not] mean that we were a new nation or a different Nation of Islam in America. He did not mean that we were a new nation or a different Nation of Islam from the Universal Nation of Islam, but he meant that this body represented the lost members from the Universal Nation of Islam.

Christ is the living body of righteous people who have been blessed with the Divine Truth that has the power to give life to

the innocent and the oppressed
which has the power to kill the
wicked.

Human beings need law
(Discipline).

"Womb" is a symbolic word that
means a place where something
is growing and developing until it
reaches its full development in
that particular womb.

Men and women who cannot
live by anything but law are
described in scriptural language
as animals that have to live
under the power or rule of

instincts. When the originator created the world he put some things under the law of instincts (natural law).

The number "6" is an esoteric number standing for materialism. It means that when materialism takes over in religion, the truth is that religion starts to die.

Knowledge is a sun, a mental sun; a sun for the mind of the people. Knowledge enables us to walk about in dark areas because we have knowledge of the dark areas.

The kindergarten language of the Christian church is what has ruled the majority of the people until today.

Apply wisdom to correct the world. Children need an image and they also need a parent that will help them mold their own image in the right shape and form.

Both the New and Old Testament speak the truth. You have to understand the symbolic language to understand the truth.

Growth goes vertically and horizontally and the first thing that a person must do is more upward. Moral growth is upward growth.

The mission of the Nation of Islam is to restore the total man, the total life, the total community.

The teachers of Christianity have fooled the whole world.

Fantasizing and hallucinating in religion is drunkenness.

Nation of Islam (Body of Christ) is formed to respond to wisdom, knowledge and understanding.

All life comes from out of the earth.

If you want to keep your marriage safe and sound and if you want to keep a good relationship do not start hiding things from each other, do not start lying to each other and do not start beating around the bush. Be open and fair with each other. Keep the light on in your house and do not hide anything from your husband or your wife.

When male and female marry they become one. In order to keep that kind of strong union, you have to live together as one that is, do not hide from yourself. If you hide things from your mate, you are hiding things from yourself. This will lead to great trouble.

If you have trouble in your marriage; you should call the two family heads together; the father and the mother from both sides, if it is possible.

When you marry and have children, you are taking on the role of Adam and you are responsible for the proper growth of society.

IX

America

Prophet Muhammad **(PBUH)** is the leader of the Ummah for America and the world.

I have great respect for the president of the United States.

Americans must realize that things are getting worst in the world due to our government's actions.

Protest and violence will come to the United States if fairness is not given to all people in our nation.

The Muslim world is in bad shape. American Muslims must be excellent examples.

The American Muslim community is evolving—it's getting better.

We—Americans must stop infighting.

Only the Quran can solve America's problems.

Don't let America pull you away from your Islam.

Islam is freedom, justice and
equality.

People want to be together
because of the goodness of their
hearts.

Let's become a fraternity of
friends; protect each other. That
is the real good neighbor policy.

To be a good Muslim—Christ
like; you must be open minded
and big hearted. Accept
everyone in the world that is
suffering.

America is a country of many nationals: it is a good time for Muslims.

Democracy is a watered down form of sharia.

Allah wants us to see that humans are one.

Everyone is born a Muslim; it is a better word or term than human.

Americans are dying from the lack of spiritual growth. We must have a moral revolution in the United States.

God is our savior and salvation. He never runs out of mercy.

What challenges us the most is corruption.

The environment of the United States almost shuts out the natural environment of God.

Our attention must be drawn to God; not man; not America.

Freedom should begin with the most useful part of life; the betterment of the natural environment.

In America—freedom started with the intellect.

The mind is the true human identity.

Knowledge and good character are the building blocks of an advanced society.

Moral life is intelligent life.

True freedom is based on morality; this is missing in America.

We want freedom for our intelligence.

Our freedom in the United States in reference to African-Americans is a reaction to our experience in this country.

Freedom is not being rude, vulgar, and ugly. That is not true freedom—this type of freedom is for the ignorant.

Our greatest hold back is separation from our traditions.

We must appreciate human life.

We must put pressure on the society that is denying us our human rights.

We must take responsibility in writing our own [African-Americans] history.

Stand up in your independent mind; that is Muslim. If you do this you will be free in America. Voting doesn't make you free.

Muslims—evolve for the good of all people. This is the high place for our people. But, don't be arrogant.

Language is powerful; we must be very careful of what we say to the people.

Language can empower or enslave the people; America knows this.

The Honorable Elijah Muhammad never had a problem with me teaching traditional Islam; it was our community—the membership.

The Nation of Islam under my father [The Honorable Elijah Muhammad] was an international organization. You did not know; but the white men knew.

We have our own "school of thought" in Islam in America. I respect the "school of thoughts" of others; but, we are not Saudis, Arabs, or Persians. We are African-Americans.

Minister Farrakhan is my brother and friend; our families are tied together. Differences should not make enemies. In the final analysis, we are Muslims.

European and Christianity created colonialism in the Muslim world. That is, they pushed their culture on us and

forced us to accept their way of
thinking. This is the root of
Muslim hurt and anger towards
the West. This issue cannot be
ignored.

I am not nor will I ever be a
spokesperson for Muslims
outside of the United States. My
job is to speak and fight for our
people.

I recommend that all of our
political leaders should read the
Quran. If Thomas Jefferson read
it; why can't you?

The president, senators and congress people need "Taqwah." They need to have and purity of the spirit, respect for superior authority and a sense of responsibility to authority and a moral commitment to do the right thing.

Americans must understand the concept of Jihad. Jihad means struggle; it is the constant effort in the way of righteousness, excellence, and community service under God.

X

Other Books

The Affirmations of the Honorable Elijah Muhammad: Leader of the Nation of Islam, Vibert and Michelle Muhammad

The Sayings of Imam Warith D. Mohammed, Vibert Muhammad, Michelle Muhammad and Hatim Hamidullah

The Wisdom of The Honorable Louis Farrakhan: The Reminder, Vibert and Michelle Muhammad

Clara Muhammad and Sisters of Islam: Comfort and Support, Michelle Muhammad

Inside The Nation of Islam, Vibert
Muhammad

The Honorable Silis Muhammad:
Statements to the United Nation on
Human Rights and Reparations, Vibert
and Michelle Muhammad

Malcolm X and Muhammad Ali: Plain
and Simple Truth, Vibert Muhammad

The Pullman Porters of Winter Park,
Florida Vibert Muhammad

18731706R00062

Made in the USA
San Bernardino, CA
27 January 2015